THIS WALKER BOOK BELONGS TO:

_____

_____

_____

For Josie

First published 1993 by
Walker Books Ltd
87 Vauxhall Walk
London SE11 5HJ

This edition including DVD published 2007

2 4 6 8 10 9 7 5 3 1

© 1993 Lucy Cousins
The author/illustrator has asserted her moral rights

This book has been typeset in Palatino
with Tiepolo punctuation

Printed in China

British Library in Cataloguing Publication Data:
a catalogue record for this book
is available from the British Library

ISBN: 978-1-4063-0822-8

www.walkerbooks.co.uk

Noah's Ark

Retold and illustrated by
Lucy Cousins

WALKER BOOKS
AND SUBSIDIARIES
LONDON · BOSTON · SYDNEY · AUCKLAND

A long time ago there lived
a man called Noah.
Noah was a good man,
who trusted in God.

There were also many wicked people in the world. God wanted to punish the wicked people, so he said to Noah...

" I shall make
and wash all
Build an
and all

a flood of water
the wicked people away.

ark for your family
the animals."

Noah worked   for years

and years   and years...

to build the ark.

At last the ark was finished.

Noah and his family
gathered lots of food.

Then the animals came,
two by two...

two by two...

into the ark.

When the ark was full
Noah felt a drop of rain.

It rained   and rained

and rained.   It rained ...

for forty days and forty nights.

The world was covered
with water.

At last the rain stopped
and the sun came out.
Noah sent a dove to
find dry land.

The dove came back with
a leafy twig.
"Hurrah!" shouted Noah.
"The flood has ended."

But many more days passed
before the ark came to rest
on dry land.

Then Noah and all
the animals came
safely out of
the ark…

and life began again on the earth.